The Tao of Millenial Money: Make More, Spend Less, and Life a Better Life

Disclaimer

This is a work of opinion and the information in this work is for educational and entertainment purposes only and does not constitute specific, individualized, or tailored financial advice in any way, shape, or form. No guarantee or warranty of any kind is associated with the information contained in this work. Please consult your tax, financial, legal, and psychic advisors, or any other professional you might consult, before following any of the ideas in this book.

Inspiration

I am writing this work without specifically referring to any other specific work on personal finance and investing. However, some of these bits of wisdom may resemble similar things others have suggested – but not on purpose. There are only so many ways to become financially free using legally available opportunities. My goal is to repeat nothing that has been said before the exact same way in any other work. When I talk about people's need to have multiple streams of income, about the need to consider real assets, or buy assets, or think about passive income, these are my thoughts, inspired by innumerous works by myriad authors and personalities. Names that come to mind include Robert Kiyosaki, who I think is a genius in inspiring others to think outside the box, Benjamin Graham, Jim Cramer, Warren Buffet, Harry Browne, everyone on *"Shark Tank"*, Marcus Lemonis, Felix Dennis, David Bach, Dave Ramsey, Tim Ferris, and a million others. My heroes consist of those who can take their entrepreneurial drive and develop platforms that can change the world through cascading (serial) entrepreneurship. Names that further inspire my thinking in this regard are Richard Branson, Jeff Bezos, and Elon Musk. I'd work for any of them just for the learning opportunity itself, and recommend that you consider doing the same if ever given the opportunity.

Dedication

This book is dedicated to *the Precariat*, a term I did not invent but which I feel best describes the millennial generation. Born of hope, inheriting a constantly changing world, with great possibilities in the decades ahead but existing in an ever more complex and precarious world of credit scores, rising costs, job insecurity, and stagnating wages that threatens personal financial calamity with the slightest of financial shocks. My hope is to reduce such risk and increase the Precariat's financial awareness with the bits of wisdom in this work.

A Full Bucket Begins with a Single Drop

Translation: Before you can make a lot of money, you must make "some money." Before you can define what "some money" means, you have to have something of value. Here let's term earning something of value as income. This means something with value (with worth) is *coming in*. When it comes to investing, everything matters – costs, fees, dividends, interest, money coming in and money going out. Understand that you can't get to be a millionaire without having a million dollars – technically, a million one dollar bills. Each of those dollar bills is 100 cents or 100 pennies worth of value. One penny less and a millionaire is no longer a millionaire.

Summary: When it comes to building wealth, every single penny/cent counts. Don't be afraid to start small.

Begin Before the Sun Rises Again

Translation: The most important ally you have in investing is not how much you invest. It's time. More specifically, it's how long you can invest and grow wealth before you need to begin withdrawing from your accumulation. You can ready plenty of books and articles on the magic of time and compounding returns so I won't cover the nitty gritty details here. Suffice it to say, you can always potentially earn more money, and you can always potentially chase higher returns, but you'll never be able to create more time. At least not in the general sense. Use time to your advantage and start investing, no matter how small, today.

Summary: Don't wait to start investing. Even in the smallest amounts. You'll never get more time.

Cut the Grass When It Grows Too Fast

Translation: If you think of your investments as a carefully tended lawn, then if things go right, your investments will grow, just like a lawn would with water, sun, and care. Just like you would cut the grass when it gets too high and starts looking ragged, don't let your earnings grow too fast without cutting back and putting some of that money aside to use when the "grass" goes through a tough time. People who get burned in public markets often fly too close to the sun, letting greed convince them that a growing investment will keep growing forever. Use hard-and-fast rules to frame your investing and to make profit-taking decisions. Think of your harvested profits as just that – sun, water, and care set aside to use when things go south – in technical terms, you should "rebalance" your investments to retain your risk tolerance. Doing so is one way to improve the odds that you'll keep the "lawn" looking great in the long term.

Summary: What goes up real fast tends to come down real fast. Especially in the world of public financial markets. A small profit is always better than a loss.

Don't Sell When the Market Stalls are Full

Translation: Markets don't go up forever. There will be times when the markets are tanking and all seems lost. The tendency for most people is to run for the exits. Panic and Sell! Panic and Sell! Why does everyone do this? Down markets are like a store putting good items on sale. Do you want to buy them when they are cheaper to purchase or when they are more expensive? Cheaper, of course! So, if you believe in the value of your investments, stay in the markets when going gets tough, only invest what you can afford to lose, and harvest your gains as I have mentioned previously. Then, you'll be in a good place to buy when things are cheaper and sell later when markets recover. The 120+ year history of the US Stock Market shows that, although the time it takes to fully recover is different, the market has always recovered from every historical crash!

Summary: If you've harvested gains (cut the grass) and have money on the side in cash, down markets can be a great time to buy. They are a terrible time to sell!

Every Now and Then, A New Chapter Begins

Translation: Markets and particular investments don't tend to go up forever. Individual investments, whether stocks, bonds, commodities such as gold, or even real estate, can go up real fast, but they can also go down real fast too. Just ask people who bought real estate at the top of the market in 2006/2007. There is a saying that I've heard from Wall Street giants, although I'm not sure who originally created the saying. It goes something like this: "You won't go broke making a profit." If you are lucky enough to own a hot investment, take some profit. If it keeps going up, you'll have made money to invest in other areas. If it goes down though, you'll be glad to have a profit to show for it. And then don't forget to reinvest some or all those gains, perhaps in a different asset class altogether.

Summary: The name of the game is "Buy Low and Sell High". Wall Street markets are indeed a casino, and only those who can walk away from the table when they are up will be winners.

Find Your Path and Follow It

Translation: Financial and investment advice is everywhere, even here. You'll find all kinds of suggestions, mostly about investing in stocks and bonds, some about investing in commodities or real estate, others about alternative or exotic investments. What should you invest in? If you get into investing, over time, you're likely to find investments that you are interested in. You may dig in, take a deep dive, learn as much as you can and keep learning. Other people's investing advice is based on two things: 1) what has worked in the past and 2) what has worked for them. Find what works for you. And then become an expert in it. That expertise will increase your investing IQ.

Summary: Do your own research and pick the investments that you like and enjoy. You'll be a better investor for it.

Grass will Always Look Greener, Anywhere but Here

Translation: Markets don't rise or fall in tandem. Different sectors, different asset classes, different types of investments will be hot, others will be warm, and some will be cold. Market leaders change with time. One sector or asset class will look unstoppable – it's almost always an illusion. Money moves, especially big money. It doesn't like to stay in one place for a long time. As a small investor, as I assume most millennials, college students and recent college graduates reading this work are, you will suffer from information asymmetry compared the institutional and sovereign investment world. By the time many smaller investors move their money into the hot sector/asset of the time, that sector tends to lose funds and momentum as larger investors reallocate to new sectors that can be bought at a low price.

Summary: Be careful chasing returns. Investments that are too hot frequently leave small investors burned.

Have a parachute in reach, always

Translation: Most people make their money primarily from a job. However, the social contract of the mid-twentieth century, the lifetime job that was central to the American dream for decades, no longer exists in the waning years of the first quarter of the 21st century. Even if it does, wage growth is uneven and income, even within the same occupation, is filled with inequality. Private organizations hire and fire employees at will, and for almost any reason desired. It is well-known that most extremely successful people do not make their income from one job – rather they frequently have multiple streams of legitimate income. Some have second jobs, some have hobbies that supply small amounts of income, some invest, some are in real estate, some have blogs, some develop websites, some receive royalties. Find a way to gain a second stream of income in addition to gainful employment or other form of occupation, no matter how small this stream begins. And then deploy it wisely.

Summary: Expand your income potential. Begin pursuing a second line of income, no matter how small, today. And then start working on another line of income.

It's A Fool's Errand to Time Feelings

Translation: When the crash or correction in an investment or group of investments begins, the most sophisticated sell first. The less sophisticated stick things out until they reach a point where the loss is too great and then they sell at a significant loss. The most unsophisticated investors wait and wait during a correction, thinking that things will go back up, and will return to where they are. They tend to wait until it looks like their investments will keep going down forever. Sometimes, they throw in the cards and sell, just when everything looks terrible. Which is usually when the market begins to turn around – and when they have sold at such a great loss that recovery is unlikely, at least in the near term. Research shows, time and time again, humans are terrible at predicting markets and market timers are more wrong than they are right. No one can reliably time markets. Keep in mind that market swings are affected by how people feel, and investor psychology can never truly be predicted with certainty in advance.

Summary: Avoid trying to time markets and use sound judgement and/or logic rules to make your investment decisions.

Jump in When the Water is Cool

Translation: Once upon a time, baseball cards were hot. I mean scorching hot. People made and lost fortunes of real money buying and selling mass-produced cardboard relics. The people that made the money were the people that had old or increasingly in-demand cardboard with the names of well-known stars on the front. The people that lost money were the people like me that bought a Jose Canseco rookie card for $120 US dollars in 1990 and watched it depreciate to $25 US dollars by 2010. When it comes to individual investments, there is a time when things are heating up and the time to buy is right. There is also a time when things are too hot or conversely, when things are too cold. Finding diamonds among common rocks is not easy. But it can be done. Use megatrends to your advantage and conduct your own research into areas/things that you anticipate will be increasing in demand with time.

Summary: Timing markets is a sucker's game. Doing research and finding fundamental reasons for an investment to increase in demand is the name of the game.

Keep Cutting the Cords that Bind

Translation: One nearly certain way to lose money in the long run is to have a high level of expenses. This is as true in life as it is in investing. It's easy to spend money. There's no skill required. It's harder to spend money wisely. And harder still is earning it. Hardest of all is making it without earning it, since money made with investments is not considered "earned" for tax purposes. Reduce the expenses that are associated with your investments. Try not to use high cost brokers, save on transaction costs wherever possible, and if using mutual funds, ETFs, or other expense-generating investments, focus in on costs and minimize these wherever possible. There are brokers out there that have free investment accounts and free trading of (albeit limited) investment opportunities. Research your options to save today, tomorrow, and for as long as you invest. I suggest researching the analysis that Jack Bogle has generated as a start in this educational process.

Summary: Investment costs can be a significant drag on your profit potential, much more than you might think. Minimize wherever possible and never invest without considering these outflows.

Living Well is More About What Leaves Than What Comes In

Translation: Everything that matters financially in life is about expenses. If you want to be rich, why is that? So that you can afford to live the life that you want, pursue the passions that you enjoy with the time that you have on this earth? Help others live their ideal life? Why do you need to work to make money, or need more money, or want to invest to make a lot more money? Is it because the things you want to do, or the lifestyle you want costs a lot? If so, then it's the cost holding you back, not the money you have. Want to live in a mansion with an oceanfront view? It costs a lot. What if it cost only a little? What if all the things you wanted or were passionate about cost only a little. I can't guarantee that you can get exactly what you want for a lot less, but most things (housing, health care, education, food, entertainment, you name it) can be found for less than you might imagine, sometimes a lot less, and usually somewhere else. Realize that you make a choice everyday – to keep living the life that you've arranged for yourself. Know that the world is filled with opportunities, but they come at a cost other than just money. Organize your life around minimizing expenses, whatever they are and wherever you are, so that you can get more out of life.

Summary: You'll never be rich enough if you buy into escalating prices. Control your expenses and costs first and foremost.

Money Will Be Your Boss, If You Let It

Translation: Most people fall into the trap of working to make payments to someone else – a bank for their mortgage, financial companies for credit cards, the doctor, the hospital, the insurance company, the electronics store, and on and on. Not to mention paying a significant chunk of change first to the IRS and state or local governments for a cut of all wages and income. Many of these expenses could be reduced (even in the case of taxes, reduced legally). I find Robert Kiyosaki's books most inspirational on the topic of breaking out of the rat race, but read up on making your money work for you from as many sources as you can and then start working on making it happen. Start today. This is a marathon, not a sprint.

Summary: Debt and owing is a double-edged sword. When used for growth potential (education, sometimes real estate, sometimes starting a business) it can cut through the fog and open opportunities. When used for dumb purposes, like buying unnecessary junk, it can cut you to pieces.

Never Confuse the Wedding for the Marriage

Translation: Nothing, and I mean nothing, causes people to open their purse-strings like a wedding. Budgets are frequently blown out of the water for a half-day (or less) party. I mean, the dress, the entertainment, the decorations, the food, the photographer, the venue, the planner, the cake...you get the point. Emotion frequently overrides common sense and people spend absurd amounts of money for these things. Plus, rings, a honeymoon, and a host of other overpriced wedding-associated costs. Why do so many people get divorced? A lot of them confuse a wedding with a marriage. And I'm especially talking to millennials, college-aged and recent college graduates. You probably have no real idea what you want out of life or what you really need in a partner, even if you think you do. No need to rush into marriage - if you're dating, just keep dating. Marriage is an economic and social contract. It is not a declaration of love. Love doesn't require a ceremony or material goods. Be smart about wedding planning, never confuse a party with a lifetime of occasional ups and many (many) downs, and for the love of all this is holy in the universe, never, ever go into debt for a wedding.

Summary: A wedding is not an investment. It is a party that you throw for everyone else if you are the one getting married. You can still have a great time and a party without going into debt to do it.

Only Growth Gets One Above the Thicket

Translation: There is a lot of financial advice out there on what to do if you have debt but want to invest. The advice is all over the place. Some say pay off all debt before investing. Others say pay off high interest debt before investing. Still others say split your money between paying off debt, saving, and investing. Since there's so much advice out there, let me throw in my opinion as well. I believe that our society depends on spending for economic success. Everything depends on consumer spending, aka consumption. So, although there are extreme savers who can resist this temptation, invest nearly all of their income and retire at age 30, you'd probably not be reading this book if you were one of them. I believe that some money must go towards growing wealth no matter how much you owe. This does not mean that you should not pay off debt. It means that you should be saving and investing while paying off debt. Yes, it may take longer to pay that debt off. But, spending behavior is largely set by the mid-20's and the most important factor in investment success is time. You can always try to make more money – you'll never be able to get back time that was lost, and the compounded returns your investments could have provided.

Summary: Don't choose between paying off debt and investing. Do both. And stop getting further in debt.

Prepare for Turbulence in Advance

Translation: When one gets into investing, obviously, the goal is to have great returns, great growth, and increased wealth. However, always remember that good markets go bad every so often, hot sectors rotate, and money moves. There are some investments that are considered safety assets. There are many different types of investments that qualify for this term, but one example frequently touted is gold, although there are many others depending on whose advice you are receiving. Most experts recommend having some investments in such safety assets, but only a small component of one's investment portfolio. The goal of such investments is not to achieve great returns – actually, I am not sure it is right to really call them investments. Their purpose is to serve as insurance by theoretically providing a positive return when other assets are going down and dropping in value. Just as you wouldn't spend all of your money on conventional insurance, don't spend too much money on safety assets. Most experts recommend something like 4-6% of portfolio (a collection of investments) assets invested for safety/insurance purposes.

Summary: Safety assets act as insurance in a collection of investments. Most experts recommend having some safety assets but not more than about 5 percent of the total amount invested as a general rule-of-thumb.

Question All Free Financial Advice

Translation: There is a lot of free financial advice out there. News channels frequently have financial websites that offer articles and blog entries from "experts" on how to easily save more money, how to easily save for a down-payment, how to easily live on $10 a week, and so on. Most of these articles and reports are absurd and treat readers as if they are 8-year old's. Articles that tell you how to save an extra $500 dollars a week and such are useless and generalized beyond reality. They generally provide no actual details, beyond the typical "stop drinking that daily expensive coffee from the expensive coffee store" or "don't eat lunch out" advice. My recommendation is to find a way to make more money from your investments to cover eating lunch out and having that coffee. Life is short, better smell the flowers while you can. Motivate yourself to find a way to cover these splurges with your newfound interest in investing – it can be done. In addition, that expensive coffee that you can't give up might lead to more productivity at work than would otherwise be the case, potentially generating opportunities that might not exist if you avoided that caffeine jolt altogether. In addition, question any advice about owning any specific investments, such as individual stocks and bonds, etc.

Summary: Do your own investment research and make your own decisions. Most free financial advice is less than useless and (I believe) in some cases, can be harmful.

Real Estate Means Forever

Translation: There's a lot of advice out there on the American dream. Supposedly, it involves a house (and perhaps a fence and some grass and so on...). However, the situation with real estate is not so simple as it once was. Homes are no longer constructed the way they once were, handcrafted with solid wood materials, real stone, crafted brick, and with an eye for detail. Modern homes are frequently mass constructed, using cheap labor, materials like OSB and plywood, under-insulated, and with poor fit and finish. The goal is frequently get it up and get it sold, much less than do it right. Of course, there are exceptions, but these are rare and generally custom (which means expensive). And that can mean more maintenance costs, a lot more. Add to that the myriad of costs associated with home ownership: a mortgage, perhaps HOA fees that can be exorbitant, community fees that are like, but in addition to, property taxes, yard and exterior maintenance that never ends, and as usual, property taxes. In most places in the US, property taxes are forever. In the few places where property tax phases out with age or exemption, they phase back in for the next owner. This illustrates the fundamental truth of real estate, as defined by many other financial experts: real estate does not mean "real" as in tangible. I have read so many authors who have discussed this but I think Robert Kiyosaki defined this in a way I would never forget: the word "real" in "real estate" is an alliteration of the Spanish work for royal – reale. The government owns all land, forever. Buying real estate is really a lease with a different name as property taxes are due annually, and if not paid, such land and homes on it can be repossessed. These issues and many other economic pitfalls have many millennials shunning home buying and focused on renting to keep their options open. Moreover, many millennials must move where the jobs are, sometimes frequently. This is not easy to do if one must sell a home where they are now to take a job where they need to be later. Although I do believe that real estate can be part of an overall wealth building strategy, I don't think it is wise to consider any real estate as an investment, and instead, focus on its utility as a place to live from a price and time perspective. Finally, as many people saw during the great recession, one could be halfway through a mortgage and still lose their homes to foreclosure. Buying a house is voluntarily taking on great risk over a very long term.

Summary: I've bought houses and I've rented. Renting is better for freedom. Buying is better for living and customizing. Both come with significant advantages and disadvantages. Tread very carefully and thoughtfully in this space.

Spending is the Death of Possibility

Translation: Every time you make a purchase, consider wants and needs. Make sure the needs go first. Remember that wants are unlimited and there are millions of ways to go broke. Like spending money on stupid things. For example, many financial authors recommend that you never purchase luxuries. Luxuries are an example of a diminishing return good – you pay a lot more for them, but get little, if any, functional improvement over lesser-priced but well-made goods. Remember that once you've spent money, all the possibilities for what that money could have been used for are gone. Think about that each time you want to spend – is it worth it? I am not just talking here about the price.

Summary: There is an opportunity cost to spending money. That money could have been used for other opportunities.

The Thousand Mile Journey Begins with a Single Step

Translation: If you have bad spending habits, as most U.S. consumers do, start working on them now. Here is the human condition – wants will always exceed needs and both will always exceed available resources (for example, money) depending on how needs are defined individually. Wants are infinite. Therefore no one is ever satisfied – people with aspirations to be rich want to be millionaires, millionaires want to be billionaires, billionaires want to keep increasing their wealth, and so on.

Summary: Read, study, and understand the difference between making money, saving money, spending money, and growing money. Start making more, saving more, and growing more today. Not tomorrow.

Use Every Tool in the Workshop

Translation: Pay less for everything. Take advantage of every opportunity to save money on purchases and spending. Consider using the money saved toward investments. How? Use every option to save, such as loyalty programs, points on any credit cards owned, online rebate programs, coupons, sales, you name it. For example, I put all my monthly utility bills (phone, energy, water, cable, internet) on a charge card – I must pay off the balance of new charges each month. Since I must pay these charges each month no matter what, by putting them on a charge card that must be paid off each billing cycle, I automatically rack up reward points. Sometimes there is a sale on the number of points for a gift card, so I save when I get the gift card. Then I can find an online sale on an item I would like to purchase, and go through the portal of an online rebate consolidator to make the purchase of an item at an already discounted price. I then receive a certain percentage of cash back that comes in the form of a check when I've earned the minimum necessary. Be creative and be smart about every purchase. This will force you to think about what you're buying, if you really need it, and if so, how to get it for less and earn "found money" that can be invested or used to pay down debt. Make it a game, but don't "go broke saving money", as the saying goes.

Summary: Make no mistake, this is not a strategy for making money. This is a strategy for spending less money when a purchase is necessary. And my suggestion is to take the proceeds of any savings and invest half and pay down debt with the other half.

Value is More Important than Price

Translation: When considering a purchase, do not look at just the price in dollars and cents. Value is the most important parameter in my opinion. If you buy something that has a low cost, but it must be replaced frequently, or doesn't work as intended, then it also has low value. In the case of luxuries, as mentioned earlier, the value proposition is generally negative – you pay a lot more and get little in return. In other cases, however, you may pay a lot less, but get a piece of junk in return that quickly breaks, wears out, looks bad, or fits poor. Look for options that have the best value. Save every dollar that you can.

Summary: Use every free resource on the value of products to help with decision making. Be careful to avoid paid reviews which may not reveal true value.

Whole is Better than Half

Translation: If you are a millennial, or headed into the college-aged cohort, or even if you are under-40 and left school and late-nights behind a while ago, life insurance is probably not something you think about a lot. But you should think about it now. Maybe you already have a family to look out for, or maybe you are waiting for the right person to come along. Life insurance is something to think about when you are ready to retire, right? Wrong. Life insurance is something to think about when you are young and healthier than you will be later in life. Unless you find the fountain of youth and never age. For the rest of us, death is a certain consequence of being alive. Think about helping those who will still be here when you have gone ahead. More importantly, and especially if you are using a group term life policy offered as a benefit at your job, do your due diligence now and explore whole life insurance options from different mutual insurance companies. Yes, they cost far more that term policies. But the right policies build cash value that can be used when you are alive, for many purposes. Whole life might not be right for you, and any such policies should be part of a financial plan, not the entirety of it. But explore the possibilities today – there are only two ways I know of to grow after-tax money on a tax-deferred basis and *use* – not necessarily withdraw – these funds tax-free: Roth IRAs and properly structured Whole Life (sometimes called 7702) policies.

Summary: Nobody in the financial services industries has a vested interest in promoting 7702 policies if they only sell financial products for 401(k) or IRA or taxable accounts. If you find negative information on whole life, see if that information is coming from an investment company. Learn about the Infinite Banking Concept today, and see if it is worth considering. Every day that goes by is a day that will cost more if you decide to include this strategy that combines life insurance and an investment component in your portfolio.

Xtra Attention to Yourself Pays Certain Dividends

Translation: Have you ever heard the saying that "Health is Wealth"? While many people can certainly achieve material wealth and fame independently of any disability, the road to financial independence is made much more difficult for someone in poor health. Health issues require attention, which can require time and energy away from the issues associated with attaining an upward career trajectory and increased compensation, the lynchpin of the mid-century American Dream. The most successful people are healthy, or at least, can meet the mental and physical energy demands and frenetic pace that upward mobility demands. Taking care of oneself is an investment in a good life, in possibilities, and in a payoff for deferred gratification. If you are engaging in self-harmful behavior (binge drinking, smoking, or illicit drug use), stop these activities now, or accept that you will never rise above the crowd and that this book is likely of no use to you. These things are likely to shorten your life and they will certainly divert money from your bank account and investments into brief minutes of entertainment that will leave you empty and anticipating the next buzz. I have no preference for a particular diet or exercise regimen. Just start to think about what you are eating, especially chemical-loaded junk, and start to reduce your intake of such material. Similarly, I am not a big fan of marathons – just getting up and getting active in something, even occasionally, is better than nothing.

Summary: Start taking care of your health now...like yesterday. You can always try to earn more money if you are healthy. You can never get more time or turn back the clock, and it's a lot harder to get healthy again once wellness has been lost.

You don't Get a Second Act in American Life

Translation: To paraphrase one of F. Scott Fitzgerald's most famous lines, the true meaning of which is still debated today. I think Fitzgerald was on to an observation, but I believe that each of us can define it in our own way. In my opinion, Fitzgerald was trying to emphasize how important it is to be careful. Be careful in the jobs you select, in your choice of a significant other, in your relationships with people and with money. If you ruin your reputation, you may not be able to recover completely, in one sense or another. If you ruin your credit, you may be able to recover somewhat, over a period of years. And there is an opportunity cost to years of credit damage, unfortunately, even though I think it would be better if we didn't depend on credit for consumption. There are frequently exceptions to generalizations, and there are people that have fallen on hard times and come out ahead in the end. But these stories are exceptions, which mean they are not the rule. Now, while you are young, being to view the life ahead as a marathon, the goal of which is to cross the finish line – which individuals must define in their own way. One must both survive, but also use logic, skill, and luck to thrive along the way. Everyone makes mistakes, but some mistakes are much more challenging to overcome, so think about the path to come and take steps to minimize the risk of making financial mistakes.

Summary: Life is hard enough as it is, and it's only getting more complicated. Think about your future today, and know that you may have more control over your financial future than any other aspect of your life.

Zero is the Loneliest Number

Translation: Think of all the different ways in which you could deploy your capital, your income, your money. Some of those ways involve spending, and the loss of your capital forever. Others involve ways to turn a dollar of capital into two dollars, and two dollars into four dollars, and so on. Are you invested? Do you have opportunities that you have not taken advantage of to increase or build wealth? Those opportunities are currently providing you zero dollars in benefits or income. Do your due diligence, decide which path you think you would like to pursue, and then act. Time is running out.

Summary: Ideas and opportunities not acted upon will always remain unfulfilled dreams. Do your research, and then take a calculated risk. Or be satisfied with the likelihood that nothing will change.

The View from the Top of the Mountain

Translation: Everyone has their own goals in life. Financial freedom and more money don't always achieve those goals, but financial freedom does provide one important advantage: opportunity. Opportunity to spend time how one pleases, whether productively or otherwise, including having time to do nothing. Each person has their own mountain to climb to achieve their version of success. Some mountains will be taller than others. There will be more people at the bottom and at lower elevations than at the top, but many people will be trying to climb higher. I encourage you to use your success, as you climb your mountain to whatever height you aspire to, to help others on their way up. Find a way to leverage your success to help them and society. Leave this world in a better place than where it was when you entered it. Working together, we can make a difference for good. Start now. If you cannot afford to donate money, find a way to donate some time, which is generally more effective in any case. Every minute spent helping a good cause makes this world a better place.

Summary: I hope that you will use these tiny bits of wisdom to improve your financial life, even if only minimally. My only request is to leverage your success, however large or small, to help this world and the people in it in some respect. I hope you can summit your own mountain, however high it is.

www.ingramcontent.com/pod-product-compliance
Lightning Source LLC
Chambersburg PA
CBHW071203220526
45468CB00003B/1145